Dogs of the World

Discover Dog Breeds and Their Countries of Origin

Rose Brown

Published by The Crackajack Company
Imprint: Brainy Bubs
Text and concept by Rose Brown
This book is intended for educational and entertainment purposes only.
First Edition, 2026

ShihTzu

China

Did you know? Shih Tzus were royal companion dogs in ancient China.

Labrador Retreiver

United Kingdom

Did you know? Labradors are friendly and love water.

German Shepherd

Germany

Did you know? German Shepherds are intelligent dogs often used in police and rescue work.

French Bulldog

France

Did you know? French Bulldogs are small, playful dogs with big personalities.

Shiba Inu

Japan

Did you know? Shiba Inu's are alert and brave dogs from Japan.

Pekingese

China

Did you know? French Bulldogs are small, playful dogs with big personalities.

Chihuahua

Mexico

Did you know? Chihuahuas are one of the smallest dog breeds in the world.

Dalmatian

Croatia

Did you know? Dalmatians are famous for their black spots.

Belgian Malinois

Belgium

Did you know? Belgian Malinois are smart dogs often used in police work.

Poodle

France

Did you know? Poodles are very intelligent and easy to train.

Siberian Husky

Russia

Did you know? Huskies were bred to pull sleds in snowy lands.

Akita

Japan

Did you know? Akitas are strong and loyal dogs from Japan.

Corgi

United Kingdom

Did you know? Corgis are famous for their short legs and big ears.

Dachshund

Germany

Did you know? Dachshunds were bred to hunt burrowing animals.

Saint Bernard

Switzerland

Did you know? Saint Bernards helped rescue people in snowy mountains.

Australian Shepherd

Australia

Did you know? Australian Shepherds love running and herding animals.

Basenji

Congo

Did you know? Basenjis don't bark-they make a unique yodel sound.

Saluki

Saudi Arabia

Did you know? Salukis are one of the oldest dog breeds in the world.

Afghan Hound

Afghanistan

Did you know? Afghan Hounds are known for their long, silky coats.

Tibetan Mastiff

Tibet

Did you know? Tibetan Mastiffs were used to guard homes in the mountains.

Indian Pariah Dog

India

Did you know? Indian Pariah Dogs are one of the oldest natural dog breeds.

Doberman

Germany

Did you know? Dobermans are fast, alert, and very loyal.

Pomeranian

Poland

Did you know? Pomeranians are tiny fluffy dogs with big personalities.

Rajapalayam

India

Did you know? Rajapalayam dogs are strong and were once used as royal guard dogs in India.

Border Collie

United Kingdom

Did you know? Border Collies are one of the smartest dog breeds.

Loved this book?
Continue the fun and creativity with the Dogs of the World Coloring Book!
Bring your favorite dog breeds to life with bold, easy-to-color pages designed for young learners and curious minds.
Search for:
Dogs of the World Coloring Book
From the Did You Know? series by Brainy Bubs.
An imprint of The Crackajack Company

9 788169 067164

Printed at Repro India Ltd.